SOLAR AND LUNAR ECLIPSES

by Ruth Owen

WINDMILL
BOOKS

New York

Published in 2013 by Windmill Books, An Imprint of Rosen Publishing
29 East 21st Street, New York, NY 10010

Produced for Windmill by Ruby Tuesday Books Ltd
Editor for Ruby Tuesday Books Ltd: Mark J. Sachner
US Editor: Sara Antill
Designer: Emma Randall
Consultant: Kevin Yates, Fellow of the Royal Astronomical Society

Photo Credits:
Cover, 1, 5 (top left), 5 (top right), 5 (bottom), 10, 14–15, 16, 17 (bottom), 18 © Shutterstock; 6–7 © EIT, SOHO Consortium, ESA, NASA; 7 (top right) © C. Witte, NASA; 8, 21, 28 © NASA; 9, 11, 13, 17 (top), 20, 27 (top) © Shutterstock/Ruby Tuesday Books Ltd.; 19 © Luc Viatour, Wikipedia (public domain); 22 © Corbis; 23 © Oscar Martin Mesonero (OSAE), SAROS Group; 25 © Science Photo Library; 26–27 © Sancho Panza, Wikipedia (public domain); 29 © NASA, ESA, and E. Karkoschka (University of Arizona).

Library of Congress Cataloging-in-Publication Data

Owen, Ruth, 1967–
 Solar and lunar eclipses / by Ruth Owen.
    p. cm. — (Explore outer space)
 Includes index.
 ISBN 978-1-4488-8077-5 (library binding) — ISBN 978-1-4488-8118-5 (pbk.) —
ISBN 978-1-4488-8124-6 (6-pack)
1. Solar eclipses—Juvenile literature. 2. Lunar eclipses—Juvenile literature. I. Title.
 QB541.5.O94 2013
 523.3'8—dc23

                                2012005286

Manufactured in the United States of America

CPSIA Compliance Information: Batch # B3S12WM: For Further Information contact Windmill Books, New York, New York at 1-866-478-0556

CONTENTS

DAY TURNS TO NIGHT

It is early morning in the city of Varanasi, India. The Sun rises into the sky over the Ganges River. Thousands of people are waiting on the banks of the river. The dawn sky is light, but suddenly the skies become dark. The Moon has covered the Sun, blocking its light and turning day to night!

On July 22, 2009, the people on the banks of the Ganges in Varanasi experienced an amazing event—a **total eclipse** of the Sun. This amazing phenomenon was not just witnessed at Varanasi, but in many parts of Asia. In some places, day turned to night for several minutes.

From Earth, it's possible to witness eclipses of the Sun, called **solar eclipses**, and eclipses of the Moon, called **lunar eclipses**. So what exactly happens during an eclipse, and what causes these amazing **astronomical** events to take place?

That's Out of This World!

Off the southeast coast of Japan, total darkness lasted for six minutes and 39 seconds during the 2009 solar eclipse. It was the longest period of darkness that will be experienced during a total eclipse in the 21st century!

The Sun rises over the Ganges River at Varanasi.

People wait on the banks of the Ganges, just minutes before the total eclipse of 2009.

The Moon (the black disk) covers the Sun, turning day to night during the 2009 total solar eclipse.

Before we get started on the science that makes solar and lunar eclipses happen, let's take a closer look at the three bodies involved—our **Earth**, the **Moon**, and the **Sun**.

Earth is a **planet**. It's a round, rocky ball that **orbits**, or moves around, the Sun.

The Sun is the nearest **star** to Earth. This giant ball of burning gases provides all the light and heat that makes life on Earth possible. The Sun is many times larger than Earth. In fact, about 1.3 million Earths would fit inside the Sun! The Sun is also a very long way from Earth— about 93 million miles (150 million km).

The Moon is a rocky ball orbiting Earth at an average distance of about 238,855 miles (384,400 km) away. It is much smaller than Earth. About 81 Moons could fit inside Earth.

That's Out of This World!

Many scientists believe that the Moon was created when a large object—perhaps another planet— collided with Earth about 4.5 billion years ago. Rock and other materials from Earth and the colliding planet flew into space. Over millions of years, this material fused together to make the Moon.

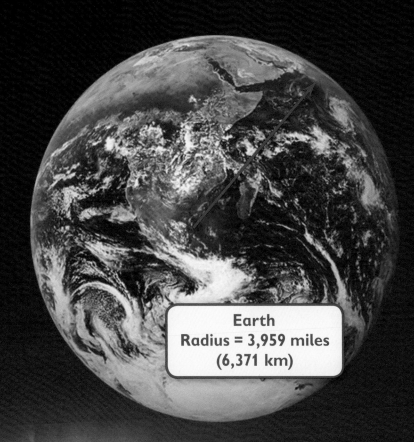

The Moon
Radius = 1,080 miles
(1,738 km)

Earth
Radius = 3,959 miles
(6,371 km)

The Sun
Radius = 432,169 miles
(695,509 km)

AROUND, AROUND, AND AROUND!

When we study eclipses, it's important to understand how Earth, the Moon, and the Sun interact with each other.

The Moon is orbiting Earth. It makes one complete orbit of Earth every 27.3 days. As the Moon orbits Earth, it follows an **elliptical**, or oval, pathway. As the Moon orbits, sometimes it is closer to Earth and sometimes it is farther away. These two points are called the **perigee** (when the Moon is closest to Earth) and the **apogee** (when it is farthest away).

Earth is orbiting the Sun. It makes one full orbit of the Sun every 365 days—the time period that we call a year.

For billions of years, the Moon has been orbiting Earth, and together, the Moon and Earth have been orbiting the Sun. This relationship between Earth, the Moon, and the Sun is one of the factors that make it possible for eclipses to happen.

This famous picture of Earth from the surface of the Moon was taken by astronauts on the Apollo 8 Moon mission.

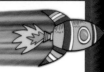

That's Out of This World!

When the Moon is at perigee, its closest point to Earth, it is 225,700 miles (363,200 km) away. When it is at apogee, its farthest point, it is 251,900 miles (405,400 km) away.

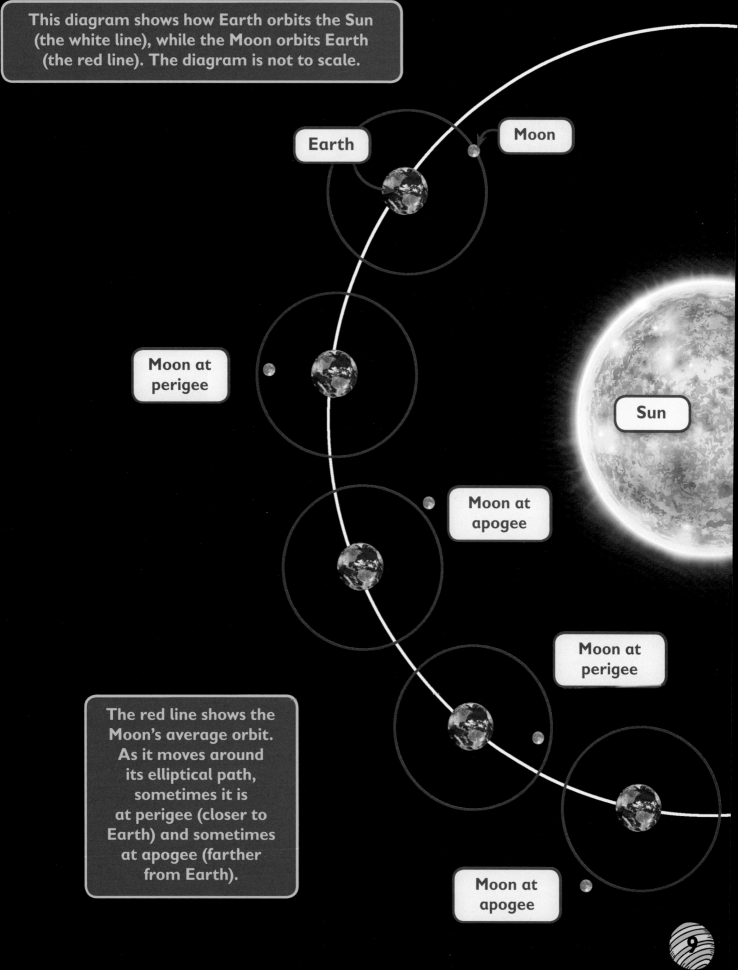

This diagram shows how Earth orbits the Sun (the white line), while the Moon orbits Earth (the red line). The diagram is not to scale.

Earth

Moon

Moon at perigee

Sun

Moon at apogee

Moon at perigee

The red line shows the Moon's average orbit. As it moves around its elliptical path, sometimes it is at perigee (closer to Earth) and sometimes at apogee (farther from Earth).

Moon at apogee

Sometimes the Moon looks like a giant white disk. This is known as a **full moon**. At other times, it becomes a thin crescent. These changing views of the Moon are phases.

A lunar eclipse can only occur when there is a full moon. So what makes the Moon's appearance change and a full moon happen?

As the Moon orbits Earth, different parts of the Moon catch the Sun's light. The diagram (right) shows the Moon making one orbit of Earth. The inner ring of small Moons shows how the Sun's light hits the Moon's surface. The outer ring of larger Moons shows what we see from here on Earth.

When we see a full moon, the Moon is on the side of Earth that is opposite from the side of Earth that faces the Sun. We get to see the whole surface of the Moon that is lit up by the Sun's light.

Full moon

Cresent moon

That's Out of This World!

The Moon has no light of its own. It looks bright because it reflects light from the Sun, just as a mirror reflects the bright light given off by a lamp or a light bulb.

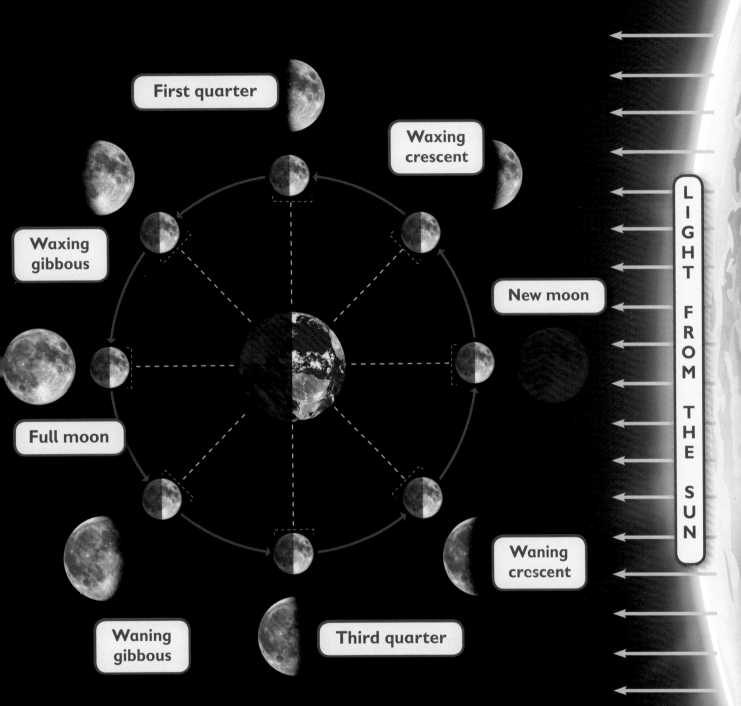

This diagram shows the Moon's phases, as seen from the northern hemisphere, during one orbit of Earth.

First quarter

Waxing crescent

Waxing gibbous

New moon

Waxing gibbous

Full moon

LIGHT FROM THE SUN

Waning crescent

Waning gibbous

Third quarter

The views of the Moon we see from Earth have names such as a full moon or a waxing crescent.

LUNAR ECLIPSES

We've looked at how the Moon orbits Earth and how its appearance changes during its different phases. So what is a lunar eclipse and why does it happen?

As Earth moves around the Sun, it casts two shadows. One is called the **penumbral shadow**, and the other is the **umbral shadow**. Sometimes, during its full moon phase, the Moon passes through these shadows (see diagram 1).

The Moon doesn't pass through the shadows on every orbit because its pathway is slightly tilted (see diagram 2). Most of the time, the Moon orbits above or below the shadows cast by Earth. Sometimes, however, the Moon's orbit takes it through Earth's shadows. This is when a lunar eclipse happens.

If a section of the Moon passes through Earth's umbral shadow, we see that section of the Moon become dark. This is called a partial lunar eclipse (see diagram 3).

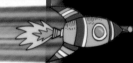

That's Out of This World!

About two to four times a year, a full Moon is in just the right position for its orbit to take it through the Earth's shadow so that we can see a lunar eclipse from Earth.

Diagram 1

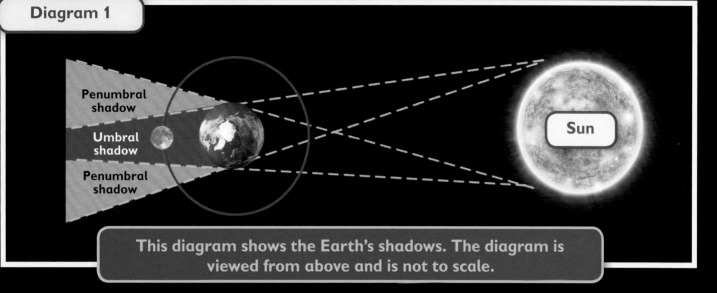

Penumbral shadow

Umbral shadow

Penumbral shadow

Sun

This diagram shows the Earth's shadows. The diagram is viewed from above and is not to scale.

Diagram 2

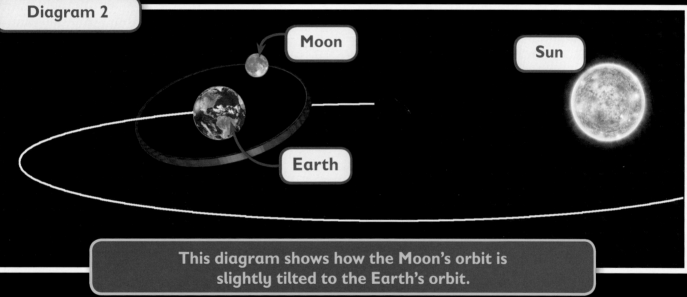

Moon

Sun

Earth

This diagram shows how the Moon's orbit is slightly tilted to the Earth's orbit.

Diagram 3

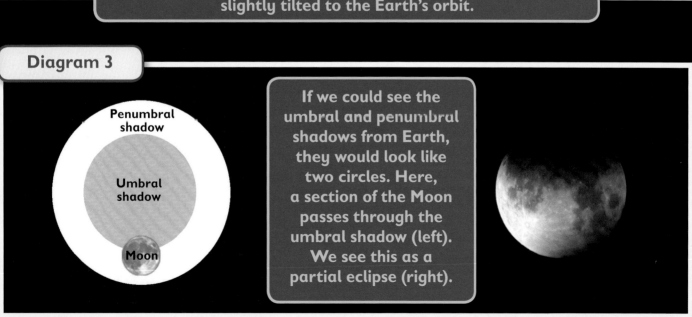

Penumbral shadow

Umbral shadow

Moon

If we could see the umbral and penumbral shadows from Earth, they would look like two circles. Here, a section of the Moon passes through the umbral shadow (left). We see this as a partial eclipse (right).

A BiG, RED MOON

Sometimes the Moon's orbit is just right for the entire Moon to pass through Earth's umbral shadow. Then, a **total lunar eclipse** occurs.

It might seem that the whole face of the Moon would turn dark during a total eclipse. In fact, something amazing happens. The Moon turns shades of red and orange.

As the Sun's light passes around Earth, Earth's atmosphere bends the light. This enables some of the light to reach the Moon and illuminate it. The Sun's light is made up of many colors. When it passes through a thick layer of Earth's atmosphere, it is mostly red light that makes it through. That's why the Moon is lit up in oranges and reds.

If Earth had no atmosphere, the Moon would appear completely black during a total lunar eclipse.

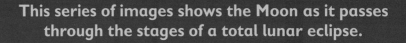

This series of images shows the Moon as it passes through the stages of a total lunar eclipse.

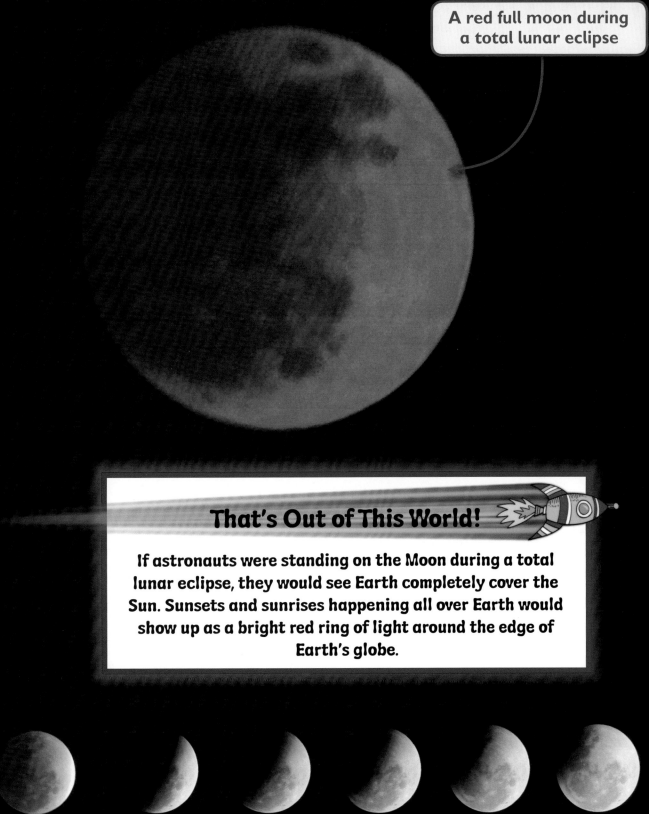

SOLAR ECLIPSES

Solar eclipses can only take place at the time of a new moon when the Moon passes between Earth and the Sun. If the orbits of Earth and the Moon are in just the right position, we see the Moon cover part or all of the Sun.

When the Moon is between the Sun and Earth, it creates a penumbral and an umbral shadow. Most of the time, the Moon's shadow misses Earth. It falls above or below Earth because the Moon's orbit is slightly tilted. Sometimes, however, the Moon's orbit is just right for its shadow to fall on Earth.

When the Moon's penumbral shadow falls on Earth, a partial eclipse happens. From the part of the world where the Moon's shadow falls, it's possible to see the Moon's dark disk cover part of the Sun.

WARNING!

You should never look directly at the Sun because it will permanently damage your eyes. When viewing solar eclipses, you should wear specially designed eye protectors.

A women wearing specially designed protective eclipse glasses

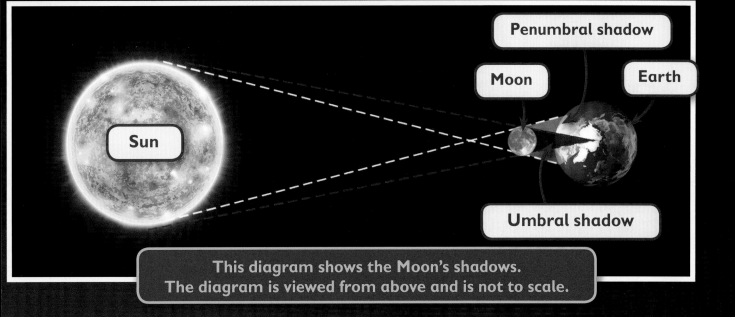

Penumbral shadow

Moon

Earth

Sun

Umbral shadow

This diagram shows the Moon's shadows.
The diagram is viewed from above and is not to scale.

A partial solar eclipse

The Sun

The Moon

THE MATH BEHIND TOTAL SOLAR ECLIPSES

Sometimes when the Moon passes between Earth and the Sun, its orbit is just right to cause a total solar eclipse. As the three bodies come perfectly into line, the Moon blocks out all the Sun's light and day turns to night on Earth!

So how is it possible that from Earth we see the tiny Moon block out the massive Sun?

The math that makes total solar eclipses possible is amazing. The Moon is 400 times smaller than the Sun. The distance between Earth and the Sun, however, is 400 times greater than the distance between Earth and the Moon. This matching up of size and distance makes the Moon exactly the right size to completely eclipse the Sun!

That's Out of This World!

The Moon's diameter is 2,160 miles (3,476 km). If its diameter were just 140 miles (225 km) shorter, the Moon would not be large enough to completely cover the Sun. We would never see a total solar eclipse!

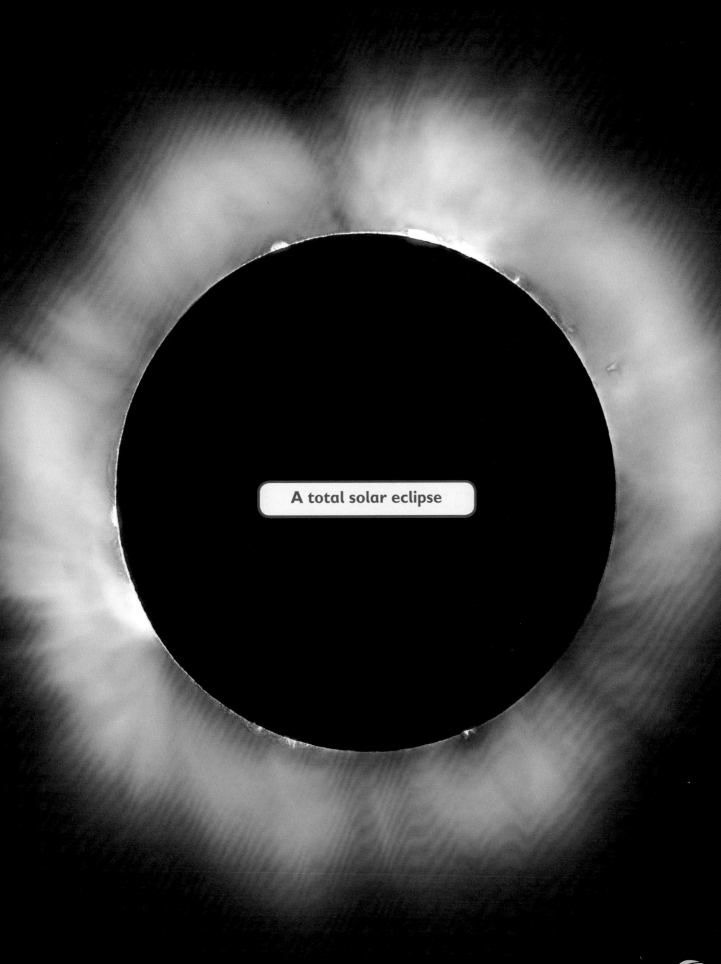

A total solar eclipse

THE PATH OF TOTALITY

During a total solar eclipse, the Moon's umbral shadow falls on just a small section of Earth. This area is called the path of totality. From this area, it's possible to see the Moon completely block out the Sun and day turn to night.

The path of totality is generally about 10,000 miles (16,000 km) long. It is usually only about 100 miles (160 km) wide, though. In order to witness a total eclipse, a person must be inside the path of totality.

A total eclipse can happen anywhere on Earth. It only happens, however, about once every two years or so. Astronomers, scientists, space fans, and TV film crews will travel across the world for the chance to see and record this amazing phenomenon!

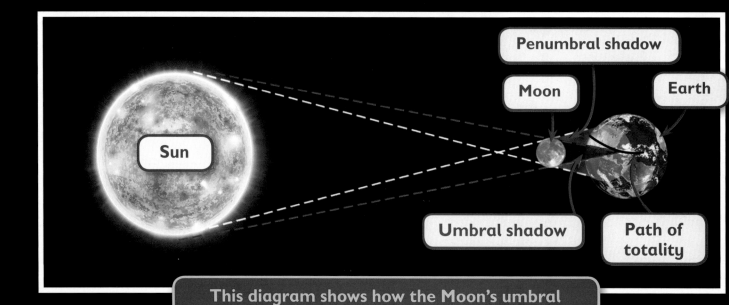

This diagram shows how the Moon's umbral shadow creates the path of totality.

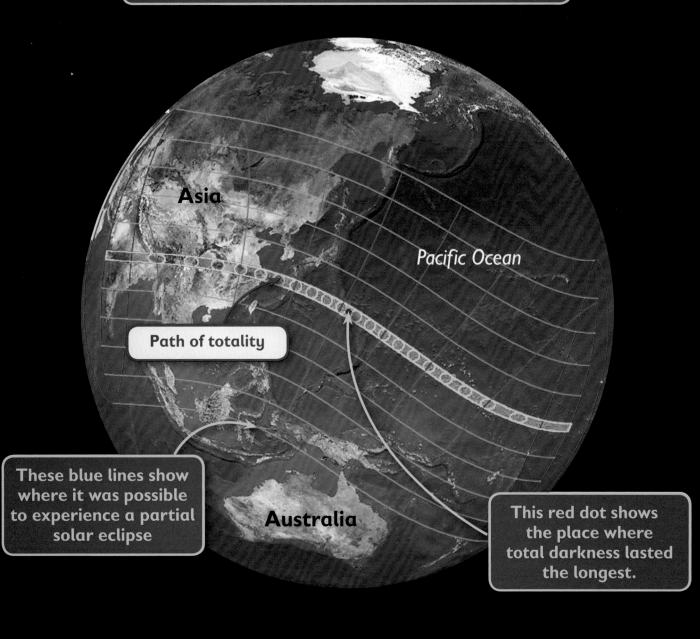

This diagram shows the path of totality that crossed Asia during the 2009 total solar eclipse.

Asia

Pacific Ocean

Path of totality

These blue lines show where it was possible to experience a partial solar eclipse

Australia

This red dot shows the place where total darkness lasted the longest.

That's Out of This World!

Because total solar eclipses can only be viewed from a very small area on Earth, it's estimated that you'd need to wait an average of 375 years to witness two total eclipses in the same place.

Most people who have been lucky enough to witness a total solar eclipse say that it is a truly awesome experience!

As crowds of people stare at the sky through special protective glasses, the dark disk of the Moon slowly moves across the face of the Sun. At the moment of totality, the Moon moves precisely into place to block out the Sun's light.

Daytime turns to night and stars appear. Birds become quiet and stop flying around. Many animals get ready to go to sleep. The temperature may drop by up to 60 degrees Fahrenheit (16 degrees Celsius).

Then after a few minutes, the edge of the Sun appears as the Moon continues on its course.

Crowds in China get ready to witness the 2009 total solar eclipse.

Baily's beads

That's Out of This World!

Just before the Moon completely blocks out the Sun during a total eclipse, beads of bright light appear around the rough edge of the Moon. The Moon's valleys and mountains are letting light through in some places and not in others. These lights are called Baily's beads after British astronomer Francis Baily, who first explained what caused them.

The Sun's Corona

As the burning disk of the Sun disappears during a total solar eclipse, the Sun's beautiful corona appears. The corona is a layer of gases that surround the Sun.

The corona is not normally visible, so total eclipses give scientists an important opportunity to study this part of the Sun. One of the mysteries they want to solve is this: How can the corona be so much hotter than the Sun's surface?

The Sun's corona has a temperature of around 1.8 million degrees Fahrenheit (1 million degrees Celsius). In places it can reach 20 times this temperature. The surface of the Sun, however, is just 10,000 degrees Fahrenheit (5,500 degrees Celsius). It's like the air around a light bulb being thousands of times hotter than the surface of the bulb!

Every total solar eclipse that occurs gives scientists a chance to try to solve the mystery of what makes the Sun's corona so hot.

That's Out of This World!

The Sun's corona extends from the Sun's surface out into space for more than 600,000 miles (1 million km).

Sometimes when a solar eclipse occurs, the Moon's disk almost blocks out the whole Sun, but not quite. This type of eclipse is known as an annular eclipse.

When a total eclipse occurs, the Moon has passed between the Sun and Earth near perigee, its closest point to Earth in its orbit. This closeness makes the Moon appear large enough to block out the Sun.

Sometimes, however, an eclipse occurs when the Moon is near apogee, its farthest point away from Earth in its orbit. This is when an annular eclipse happens. The Moon is farther away from Earth, so it is not large enough to completely block out the Sun. The Moon almost covers the Sun, but a bright ring of sunlight can still be seen surrounding the dark disk of the Moon.

An annular eclipse

Sun

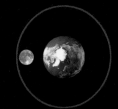

The Moon is at perigee in its orbit (the red line) —a total solar eclipse can happen.

The Moon is at apogee in its orbit—an annular eclipse will happen.

This diagram is viewed from above and is not to scale.

That's Out of This World!

The movements of our Earth and its Moon work like clockwork. Astronomers can track the orbits of Earth and the Moon and precisely predict when and where eclipses will happen for hundreds of years into the future.

An Extraordinary Event

Earth is not the only planet in our **solar system** that has a moon and experiences eclipses. In fact, there are over 150 known moons in the solar system. **Our Moon is the only one, however, that can cause a total eclipse of the Sun!**

This won't always be the case, though. The Moon is slowly drifting away from Earth at about 1.6 inches (4 cm) every year. In a billion years from now, the Moon may no longer be at just the right distance to ever completely block out all the Sun's light. This means there will be no more total solar eclipses on Earth.

We are lucky enough to be on this planet at a moment in its history when it's possible to enjoy the amazing event that is a total solar eclipse. So put on those protective glasses, look to the skies, and enjoy!

The Mars Exploration Rover *Opportunity* took these pictures of a partial solar eclipse on Mars. One of the planet's moons, Phobos, is moving between the Sun and Mars.

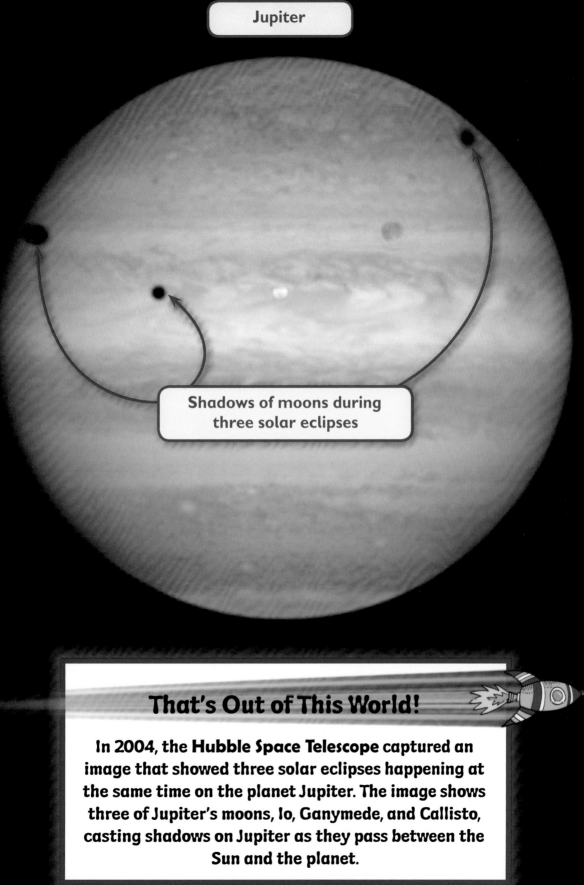

Jupiter

Shadows of moons during three solar eclipses

That's Out of This World!

In 2004, the **Hubble Space Telescope** captured an image that showed three solar eclipses happening at the same time on the planet Jupiter. The image shows three of Jupiter's moons, Io, Ganymede, and Callisto, casting shadows on Jupiter as they pass between the Sun and the planet.

GLOSSARY

apogee (A-puh-jee)
The point in the Moon's orbit when it is farthest from Earth.

astronomical (a-struh-NAH-mih-kul)
Having to do with outer space or with the science of outer space.

atmosphere (AT-muh-sfeer)
The layer of gases surrounding a planet, moon, or star.

elliptical (ih-LIP-tih-kul)
Having a rounded and slightly elongated shape, like an oval.

full moon (FUHL MOON)
The phase of the Moon in which its entire disk, or surface facing Earth, is lit by the Sun.

lunar eclipses (LOO-ner ih-KLIPS-ez)
Events in which the Moon appears darkened as it passes into Earth's shadow.

orbits (OR-bitz)
The paths that objects in space take as they circle another object, such as the Moon when it circles Earth, or Earth when it circles the Sun.

penumbral shadow (pih-NUM-brul SHA-doh)
The partially shaded outer region of a shadow cast by Earth or the Moon as it moves in front of the Sun.

perigee (PEHR-uh-jee)
The point in the Moon's orbit when it is closest to Earth.

planet (PLA-net)
An object in space that is of a certain size and that orbits, or circles, a star.

solar eclipses (SOH-ler ih-KLIPS-ez)
Events in which the Sun is fully or partially blocked from view by the Moon passing in front of it.

star (STAR)
A body in space that produces its own heat and light through the release of nuclear energy created within its core. Earth's Sun is a star.

total eclipse (TOH-tul ih-KLIPS)
An event in which an object in space passes completely through the umbral shadow of another object, or is blocked completely from view by another object, and appears darkened.

total lunar eclipse (TOH-tul LOO-ner ih-KLIPS)
An event in which the Moon passes through Earth's umbral shadow and appears darkened in shades of red and orange.

umbral shadow (UM-brul SHA-doh)
The fully shaded inner region of a shadow cast by Earth or the Moon as it moves in front of the Sun.

WEBSITES

For web resources related to the subject of this book, go to: www.windmillbooks.com/weblinks and select this book's title.

Read More

James, Lincoln. *Solar Eclipses*. Science Scope. New York: Rosen Classroom, 2009.

Morrison, Jessica, and Steve Goldsworthy. *Eclipses*. Space Science. New York: Weigl Publishing, 2012.

Olson, Gillia M. *Phases of the Moon*. Patterns in Nature. Mankato, MN: Capstone Press, 2008.

Index